QUEEN ELIZABETH II

QUEEN ELIZABETH II

The Silver Jubilee Book 1952–1977

Michèle Brown

St Martin's Press
New York

Copyright © 1976 Text Michèle Brown
Photographs Fox Photos 1928–1976
All rights reserved. For information write:
St. Martin's Press, Inc., 175 Fifth Avenue, New York, N.Y. 10010
Printed in Great Britain
Library of Congress Catalog Number: 76-29855
First published in the United States of America in 1977

Events

1926	21 April	Birth of Princess Elizabeth Alexandra Mary, elder daughter of Duke and Duchess of York
1936	11 December	Duke of York succeeds to throne as King George VI
1947	9 July	Betrothal of Princess Elizabeth to Lieutenant Philip Mountbatten RN
	20 November	Marriage of Princess Elizabeth to Philip, Duke of Edinburgh
1948	14 November	Birth of Prince Charles Philip Arthur George
1950	15 August	Birth of Princess Anne Elizabeth Alice Louise
1952	6 February	Death of George VI. Princess Elizabeth succeeds to the throne as Queen Elizabeth II
1953	2 June	Coronation of Elizabeth II at Westminster Abbey
1953–54	24 November–10 May	Commonwealth tour
1957	22 February	HRH Duke of Edinburgh given title of Prince
	Autumn	Prince Charles becomes a boarder at Cheam preparatory school
	25 December	First televised Christmas broadcast
1959	18 June–1 August	Royal tour of Canada
1960	19 February	Birth of Prince Andrew Albert Christian Edward
	6 May	Marriage of Princess Margaret Rose to Antony Armstrong-Jones (later Earl of Snowdon)
1961	21 January–2 March	Royal tour of India and Pakistan
	8 June	Marriage of Duke of Kent to Katharine Worsley at York Minster
1962	1 May–24 July 1967	Prince Charles goes to Gordonstoun
1963	24 April	Marriage of Princess Alexandra to Angus Ogilvy
	20 September–23 July 1968	Princess Anne goes to Benenden
1964	10 March	Birth of Prince Edward Antony Richard Louis
1966	1 February–7 March	Royal tour of West Indies
	2 February–29 July	Prince Charles goes to Timbertop school in Australia
1967	29 June–5 July	Queen visits Canada to open Expo '67

October–June 1970		Prince Charles goes up to Trinity College, Cambridge
1969 Summer		Prince Charles spends a term at University College of Wales, Aberystwyth
1 July		Investiture of Prince Charles as Prince of Wales
		Royal family television film for BBC and Independent Television
1970 30 March–3 May		Royal tour of Australia
1971 February		Princess Anne on safari in Kenya
September		Princess Anne wins Raleigh Trophy in the Individual European Three-Day Event at Burghley
1972 20 November		Queen Elizabeth and Prince Philip celebrate their Silver Wedding anniversary
1973 17–22 October		Queen visits Australia to open Sydney Opera House
14 November		Marriage of Princess Anne to Captain Mark Phillips
1974 13 June		Prince Charles makes his maiden speech in the House of Lords
1976 6 July		Queen visits United States for the bicentennial celebrations
17 July		Queen opens Olympic Games in Montreal
1977 6 February		Twenty-fifth anniversary of Queen's accession
7 June		Official celebration of Queen's Silver Jubilee

Introduction

On 6 February 1952 the death of George VI brought his daughter face to face with the daunting challenge of becoming 'Queen Elizabeth II by the Grace of God Queen of this Realm and of all Her other Realms and Territories, Head of the Commonwealth, Defender of the Faith'. The overwhelming enthusiasm for her as the symbol of a new Elizabethan age of peace and prosperity after the war years seemed only to increase the toughness of the challenge. Who could possibly live up to such an image? Indeed, cynics were soon prophesying that the British throne would topple as soon as the twenty-five-year-old girl showed signs of becoming an ageing matron. Yet here we are, twenty-five years later, and Queen Elizabeth II is, if anything, more popular than ever, respected, admired and trusted more than almost anyone else. How has the relatively inexperienced young woman of twenty-five years ago managed to stay so firmly in the hearts of her people?

One contributory factor must be her own hard work. Even critics of the monarchy cannot deny that the Queen does everything demanded of her and more. Others cannot praise her professionalism enough, even in relatively minor details like taking the trouble to make sure weary press photographers are given the chance of a good picture when it is obvious that so far they have been out of luck. She has even managed to tread the delicate balance between looking attractive and radiating her own special glamour without overdoing it and appearing like a starlet.

But the Queen's success is more than just that of a good professional. What comes over is her sincere dedication to what she clearly regards as not merely a way of filling in time or earning a living, but a real vocation.

Fortunately, too, the Queen seems to have the patience, and maybe something of a liking, for what is in many ways a monotonous annual routine of handshaking, tree-planting, plaque unveiling, military reviewing, polite small talk and formal meals from one Christmas to the next. Even the interest and excitement of visits abroad, to places most people can only dream of seeing, must inevitably be marred by schedules planned from minute to minute and the ever-present onlookers and press men. Even if the Queen is by temperament a person who likes routine, her dedication to the repetitive royal round should not be underestimated or under-appreciated.

The permanence represented by the Queen is in fact greatly bolstered by the consistency of her routine. Governments may come and go but the Trooping of the Colour goes on for ever and, if that gives us some sense of security in the continuity of our national life, it is no bad thing. It is essentially the Queen's role to provide that continuity, not just in this country, but in the other countries of which she is Queen, such as Australia, New Zealand and Canada, and in the Commonwealth of which she is also the head, a position quite separate from that of Queen of the United Kingdom.

The Queen's family too have helped her in her twenty-five years, partly in the straightforward sense of taking on some of the burden of royal duties—helping with foreign visits, laying foundation stones, and so on. They also give the Queen herself the secure base she needs to fulfil her role. Looking through the millions of photographs of the Queen, two things are particularly striking. One is the incredible similarity of the years and the events of every day over those years, the other is the obvious pleasure she finds in her family. It may seem a mawkish view in the twenty-fifth year since her accession, when everything seems so much more sophisticated, and people more cynical than they were then, but the Queen still comes across as very much a family woman. She is also a true animal lover, particularly of dogs and horses—which may be responsible for some subtle psychological bond with her people!

Of course the Duke of Edinburgh's part in the tremendous success of the Queen's reign—some might even call it a success still to be a reigning monarch at all—cannot be forgotten. He has the chance to speak out while his wife must remain discreet, and in this way gives the monarchy an added dimension and vitality it might otherwise noticeably lack. The Queen is fortunate to be married to an individualist who has not been swamped by his role as consort. Instead, the Duke has brought a measure of ordinary humanity to the monarchy which makes it all the more acceptable at a time when people are less inclined to sit back and offer their loyalty without very good reason.

In twenty-five years the Queen has brought the monarchy far closer to her people than it has ever been, particularly by taking advantage of the media and of faster, simpler travel. She has seen the end of the Empire and the development of the Commonwealth. The monarchy is still here and still popular, despite far-reaching social and economic change. It will be interesting to see how successfully the royal 'family firm' copes with the next twenty-five years stretching forward to the Golden Jubilee.

Princess Elizabeth at the time of her fourteenth birthday, April 1940. The Queen has always been a keen rider ever since she was given her first pony, a Shetland called Peggy. At 145 Piccadilly, her childhood home before George VI's accession, the Princess kept a large collection of toy horses. It is alleged that she once said that if she ever became Queen she would make a law forbidding riding on Sundays so that horses could have a rest

Princess Elizabeth with her nurse, Mrs Knight, on Alexandra Rose Day 1928

The young Princess Elizabeth with her mother and father, then Duke and Duchess of York, at Royal Lodge, Windsor

The royal family at Royal Lodge, Windsor, in 1942. Although George VI and Queen Elizabeth were determined to remain in London during the war, Princess Elizabeth and Princess Margaret spent most of the war years in the comparative safety of Windsor. Latterly, however, Princess Elizabeth served with the ATS

Bottom Left. Princess Elizabeth and Princess Margaret with their grandmother, Queen Mary, widow of George V. This photograph was taken during a tour of London docks on 8 May 1939. Queen Mary, who took a keen interest in preparing her grand-daughter for the responsibilities of monarchy, unfortunately did not live to see her crowned. She died on 24 March 1953, shortly before Elizabeth's coronation

August 1940. The royal sisters driving a pony and trap in Windsor Great Park

22 July 1939. The first-ever photograph of the Queen and Prince Philip together, taken when the royal family visited the Royal Naval College, Dartmouth, where Prince Philip was a cadet. Princess Elizabeth, then aged thirteen, is on the far left wearing a beret, while eighteen-year-old Prince Philip, second from the right, stands next to his uncle, the Earl of Mountbatten. Also in the picture is Princess Margaret, sitting next to her father, King George VI

An engagement picture, taken at Buckingham Palace, of Prince Philip with Princess Elizabeth and Princess Margaret. The betrothal of Princess Elizabeth and Prince Philip was formally announced on 9 July 1947 when George VI issued the following statement: 'It is with great pleasure that the King and Queen announce the betrothal of their dearly beloved daughter the Princess Elizabeth to Lieutenant Philip Mountbatten RN, son of the late Prince Andrew of Greece and Princess Alice of Battenburg, to which union the King has gladly given his consent.' (Prince Philip's mother was the sister of the Earl Mountbatten)

20 November 1947. HRH the Princess Elizabeth and HRH the Duke of Edinburgh leaving Westminster Abbey after their wedding. Prince Philip had received the title of Duke of Edinburgh only the day before. For a while after her marriage Princess Elizabeth took the surname Mountbatten, but eventually reverted to her own family name of Windsor

5 June 1952. Taking the salute at the Trooping of the Colour. Although the Queen's coronation did not take place until over a year after her accession, the round of royal ceremony and duty began at once.

Trooping the Colour, the ceremony for the Sovereign's official birthday, is almost the best known of the royal ceremonies. It began as an exercise to ensure the soldiers would recognize and follow their own colours in battle; the regimental colour of one of the five regiments of Footguards is 'trooped' through the ranks of Guardsmen. It is the only occasion in the year when the Queen appears in public on horseback, and the only time she rides sidesaddle. She wears a specially adapted skirt with the tunic of whichever regiment of Guards is being trooped, and a tricorne hat adorned with the plume of the same regiment

27 October 1952. The Queen meets Charlie Chaplin at a royal film performance in aid of charity at the Empire Theatre, Leicester Square. Nearly twenty-five years later Charlie Chaplin was dubbed Sir Charles Chaplin at Buckingham Palace

Bottom Left. 4 November 1952. The Queen, accompanied by the Duke of Edinburgh, walks through the Palace of Westminster for the first State Opening of Parliament of her reign. This was the first time the occasion was photographed. The Queen is wearing the crimson velvet Robe of State worn by her great-great-grandmother, Queen Victoria. Before Parliament is opened, Yeomen of the Guard inspect the cellars of the Houses of Parliament, a tradition going back to 1605 when Guy Fawkes was discovered trying to blow up the King

12 March 1974. The Queen, with the Lord Great Chamberlain, the Marquess of Cholmondely, after opening Parliament. She is wearing day dress and arrived by car without any of the usual ceremony because Parliament was called very suddenly at a time of national crisis

3 December 1952. The Commonwealth Prime Ministers pictured with the Queen in the throne room at Buckingham Palace after she had given a dinner for them and their wives. Left to right: The Hon D. S. Senanayaka (Ceylon); Sir Godfrey Huggins (Rhodesia); the Rt Hon S. G. Holland (New Zealand); Mr Winston Churchill; HM the Queen; the Rt Hon Robert Menzies (Australia); the Rt Hon L. S. St Laurent (Canada); the Hon N. C. Havenga (South Africa); the Hon Khwaja Nazimuddin (Pakistan); Mr C. D. Deshmukh (India)

25 December 1952. The Queen making her first Christmas radio broadcast from Sandringham, the traditional residence of the royal family at Christmas. In 1957 the Christmas broadcast was televised for the first time

Her Majesty, wearing the Imperial State crown, returns to Buckingham Palace after her coronation. She rides in the Great State Coach built in 1762 for George III and now used solely for coronations

Queen Elizabeth waves to enthusiastic crowds from the balcony at Buckingham Palace on her return from Westminster Abbey. With her are the Duke of Edinburgh, Prince Charles, Princess Anne, Queen Elizabeth the Queen Mother and the Queen's attendants

Top Left. Prince Charles, standing between Princess Margaret and Queen Elizabeth the Queen Mother, watches his mother being crowned

Left. 25 April 1953. In the hectic year between her accession and coronation the Queen snatches some relaxation in the company of Princess Margaret at the International Horse Trials at Badminton

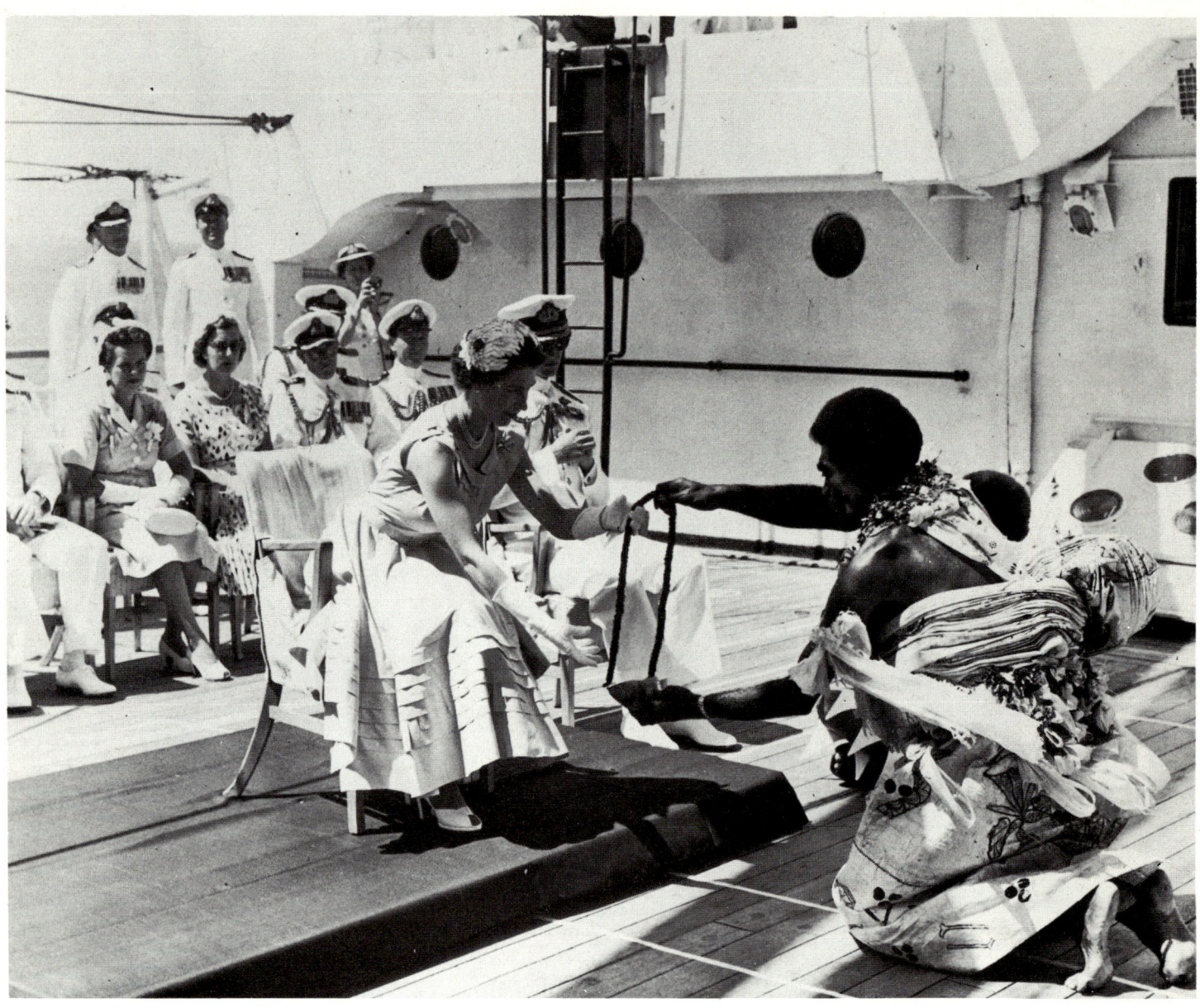

The Royal Commonwealth Tour 1953–54
Her Majesty is not only Sovereign of the United Kingdom, she is also head of the Commonwealth. As soon as possible after her coronation the Queen left on an extended Commonwealth tour in order to meet the rest of her people. In six months she visited Canada, Bermuda, Jamaica, Fiji, Tonga, New Zealand, Australia, the Cocos Islands, Ceylon, Aden, Uganda, Malta and Gibraltar

17 December 1953. On board the royal liner *Gothic*, in Suva Bay, a Fijian chief performs the traditional invitation to land

2 January 1954. At Rotorua in New Zealand the Queen and the Duke of Edinburgh were welcomed by over 20,000 Maoris at Arawa Park, their ceremonial grounds. As a sign of chieftainship Her Majesty and the Duke were presented with korowais (cloaks) made of fine flax

28 December 1953. Queen Salote of Tonga shows the Queen and Prince Philip a tortoise said to have been brought to Tonga by the English explorer, Captain Cook, nearly 200 years earlier

3 February 1954. The Queen and Prince Philip leave the *Gothic* on their arrival at Sydney for the start of their Australian visit

12 February 1954. Wild flowers are presented to the Queen at a civic reception at Katoomba in New South Wales

16 February 1954. The Queen with the then Prime Minister of Australia, Robert Menzies, after a banquet at Parliament House in Canberra. The Queen is wearing the sash and star of the Garter and a garland of tea roses on her right shoulder

22 February 1954. The Queen and the Duke of Edinburgh are greeted as they leave a civic ball given in their honour in Hobart

25 February 1961. The Queen rides on an elephant during a visit to the holy city of Benares, in India

25

2 June 1953. Westminster Abbey. The Queen has just been crowned and is wearing St Edward's Crown. The Duke of Edinburgh is the first of her subjects to make his individual act of homage. Placing his hands in hers he repeats the centuries-old formula: 'I, Philip, Duke of Edinburgh, do become your liege man of life and limb, and of earthly worship; and faith and truth I will bear unto you, to live and die, against all manner of folks. So help me God.'

9 August 1973. The Queen gets an enthusiastic reception on a 'walkabout' in the city of Bath

16 March 1954. Brisbane Exhibition Centre. The Queen seems to be the only person unaware of the unexpected approach of a little girl eager to sit on her lap. However, the young visitor is gently encouraged to give up her ambition

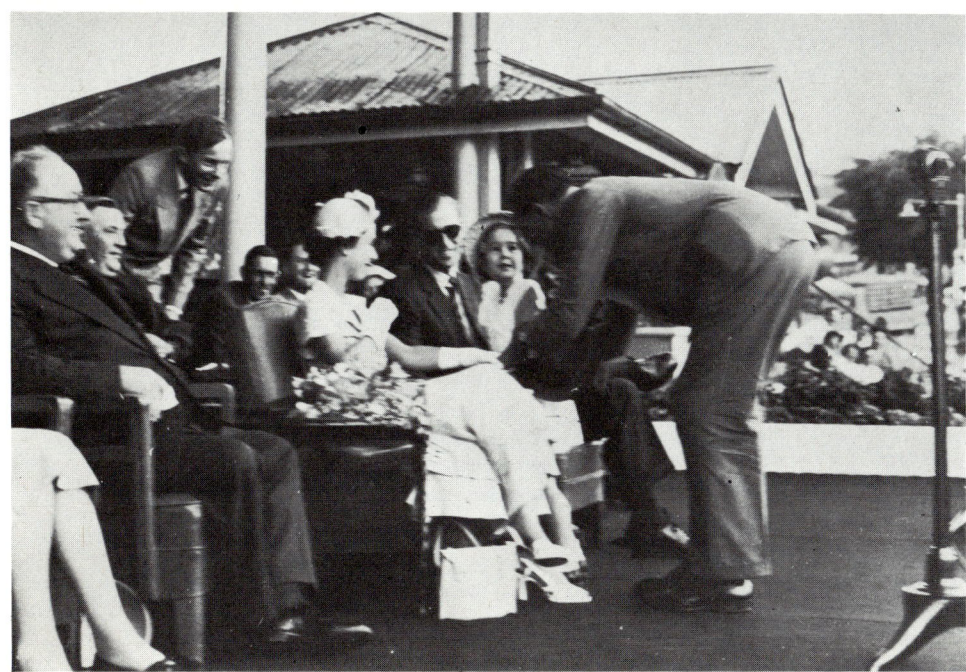

26 September 1952. King Faisal of Iraq and the Regent of Iraq (extreme right) are entertained at the Queen's home in Scotland, Balmoral. The Duke of Edinburgh, Prince Charles and Princess Anne are with them

17 March 1953. Marshal Tito of Yugoslavia was one of the first of the Queen's many foreign visitors after her accession

14 October 1954. Haile Selassie, Emperor of Ethiopia, accompanied by the Queen and Prince Philip, in an open State landau on his arrival for a two-day State visit

18 October 1955. All smiles—the Shah of Persia and his twenty-one-year-old wife, Soraya, after lunch with the Queen at Buckingham Palace

4 April 1955. Sir Winston Churchill, shortly before he resigned as Prime Minister, escorts the Queen to her car after dinner at 10 Downing Street. The Queen's white mink stole was a present from the Hudson's Bay Company of Canada on her accession

Two pictures from the Queen's tour of Nigeria in January and February 1956. On the left four-year-old Foloshade Lawson, daughter of the chairman of Lagos Town Council, presents a bouquet to the Queen. The little girl is wearing the Yoruba costume with its distinctive turban; (*below*) Her Majesty, holding a cream parasol as protection against the strong sun, waves to ranks of robed tribesmen at Kaduna

16 February 1957. The Queen's State visit to Portugal began with a reunion with the Duke of Edinburgh after his individual four-month Commonwealth tour. They are seen leaving the aircraft at Lisbon where the Duke had gone to meet the Queen

7 June 1957. HM the Queen proudly leads in her filly, Carrozza, after winning the Oaks at Epsom. Carrozza was ridden by Lester Piggott, then aged twenty-one. The Queen is an acknowledged expert in stable management and horsebreeding and registered her own racing colours in 1949

Getting away from it all with the children, at
Balmoral in September 1957

September 1959. The Queen and her family entertain President Eisenhower at Balmoral. They had previously met on the Queen's State visit to the United States two years before and also when they jointly opened the St Lawrence Seaway

5 April 1960. The French President, General de Gaulle, is welcomed to England by the Queen

June 1959. The royal family on the East Terrace of Windsor Castle

The Queen has been a frequent visitor to Canada. Before her accession she had already made an extensive tour of the country and has returned there many times. In the summer of 1959 she stayed for nearly two months when one of her many official engagements was to open the St Lawrence Seaway

October 1951. Snugly wrapped up in furs and blankets the Queen enjoys the excitement of a rodeo in Calgary, at the foot of the Rockies. The hats of Prince Philip and the other men emphasize that this is real cowboy country

18 June 1959. On her arrival in Newfoundland for the start of the Canadian tour, the Queen is presented with a bouquet by Gale Russell. Rather overcome with shyness Gale clings on to the flowers and the Queen reaches down to take them

Left. 6 July 1959. A little girl creeps through to the front of the crowd to see the Queen arrive at the Royal York Hotel in Toronto for the Provincial Government dinner

Above. The Queen and Prince Philip in a relaxed moment during the Canadian tour

The next best thing to a visit to Canada: Prince Charles and Princess Anne meet the Mounties at Combermere Barracks, Windsor

24 June 1959. At Deer Lake in Newfoundland the Queen presents the Queen's Scout Badge to Maxwell Brown. On the right an over-enthusiastic Brownie is 'restrained' by her father

The Queen's third child, Prince Andrew, was born on 19 February 1960. These pictures, of Prince Andrew aged seven months, were taken at Balmoral

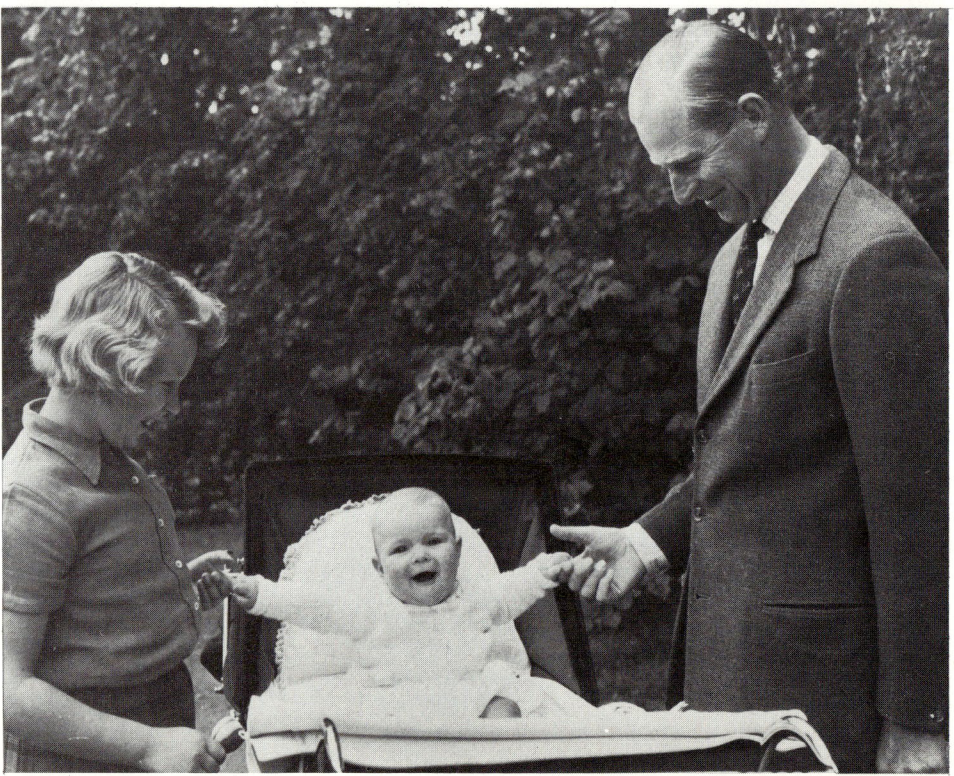

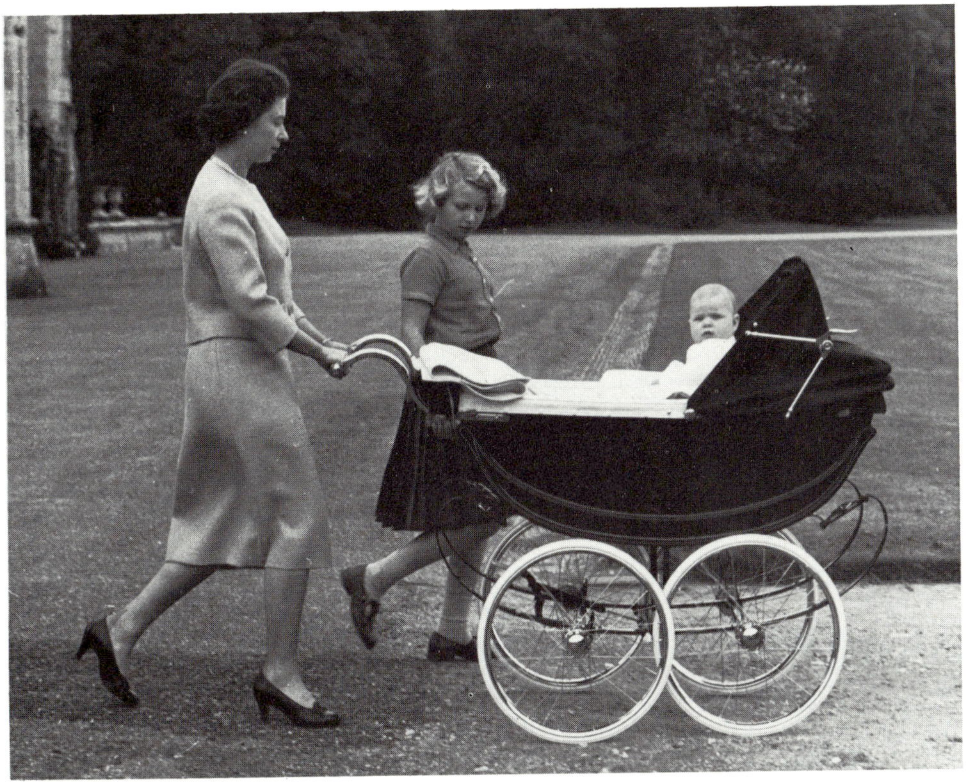

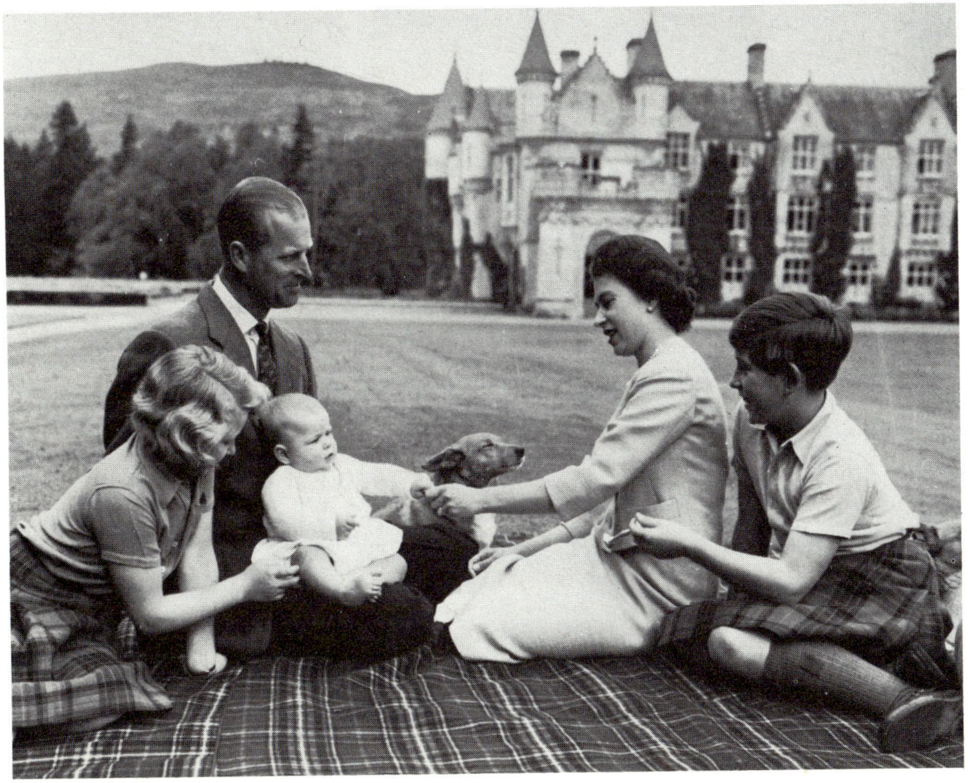

4 August 1960. The Queen Mother with her grandchildren, Prince Charles, Princess Anne and Prince Andrew, in the grounds of Clarence House on the Queen Mother's sixtieth birthday

6 May 1960. The marriage of Princess Margaret Rose to Antony Armstrong-Jones. The bride and groom leave the altar after the ceremony in Westminster Abbey. The marriage ended on 19 March 1976 when a statement from Kensington Palace announced their separation

In January and February 1961 the Queen and the Duke of Edinburgh made a six-week tour of India and Pakistan. It was the Queen's first visit to the Indian subcontinent, although Prince Philip had already been there in 1959

22 January 1961. The Queen visits the Memorial of Gandhi, Rajghat, where the Indian Prime Minister, Mr Nehru, presents her with a book on the life of Gandhi

30 January 1961. Outside the Taj Mahal the Queen draws attention to her reflection in the still water of the lotus pond. The Taj Mahal was built by the Mogul Emperor, Shah Jahan, as a mausoleum for his beautiful wife, Mumtaz. The Queen later returned to see the Taj Mahal by moonlight when it is considered to be at its most beautiful

6 February 1961 in Quetta, Pakistan. The Queen touches the head of a sacrificial sheep to signify her acceptance of the gift. The gift is offered by tribal Maliks (chieftains) and is the traditional Pathan way of welcoming a distinguished guest

The Queen dons red velvet slippers before being shown round the Taj Mahal by four barefooted guards who claim to be descended from the original guardians of the tomb

Using a ciné camera. Her Majesty is a keen photographer and originally began making films of her tours to show her children what she had seen while she was away

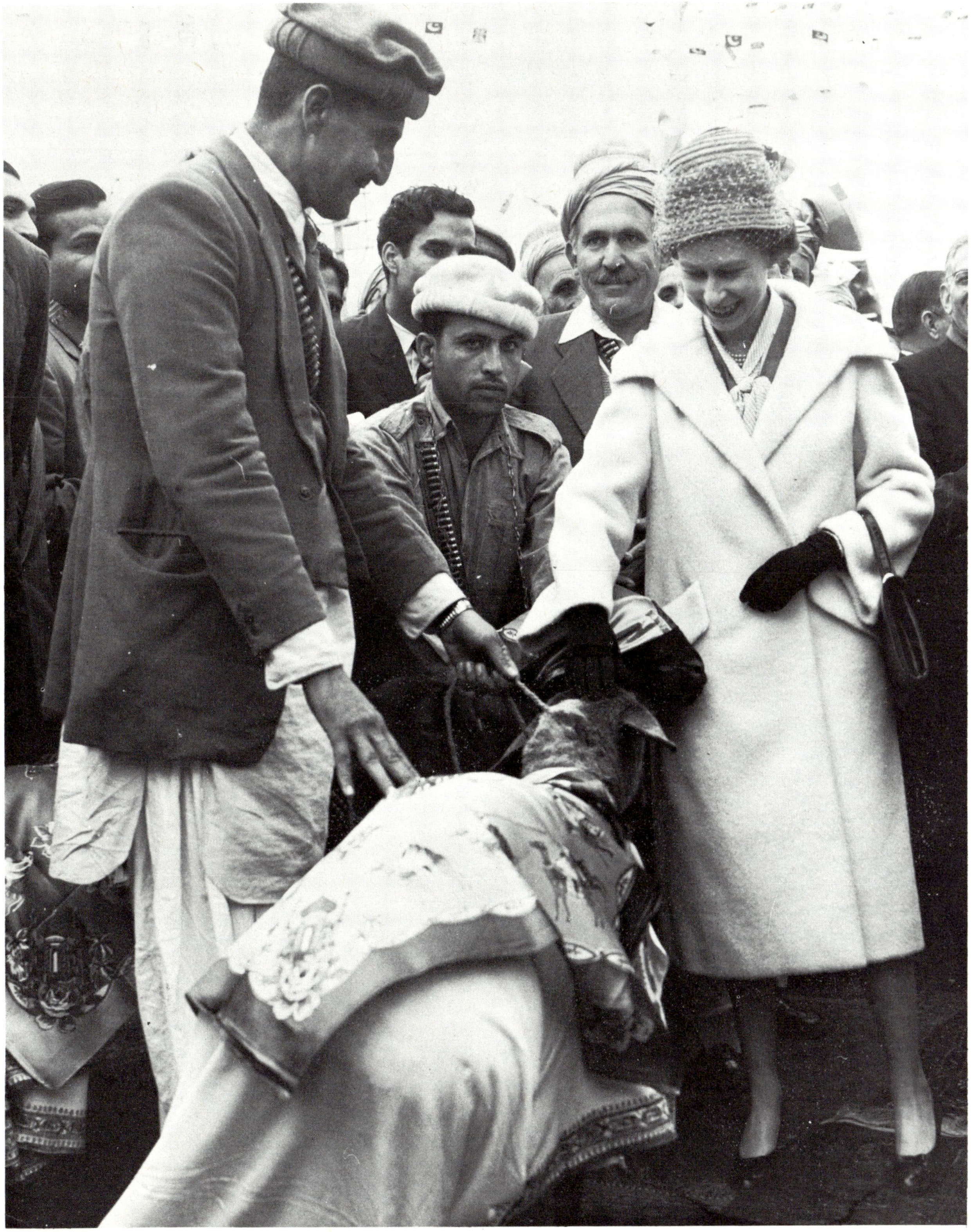

2 March 1961. On her way back from India the Queen paid a four-day State visit to Iran. The photograph shows her at a banquet in the Golestan Palace, Teheran, with the Shah and Queen Farah

6 May 1961. In the throne room of the Vatican the Queen and the Duke of Edinburgh pose for a photograph with Pope John XXIII. The magnificent tiara which supports the Queen's veil belonged to her great-grandmother Queen Alexandra

53

8 May 1961 in Venice. Four gondoliers in scarlet and white sixteenth-century livery take the Queen and Prince Philip to a dinner given in their honour at the British Consulate

25 May 1962. Her Majesty with the Bishop of Coventry, on the steps of the new Coventry Cathedral after the service of consecration. Behind them is Epstein's giant sculpture, *St Michael and the Devil*

The Queen and the regimental mascot get to know each other when the Queen inspects troops during a visit to Wolverhampton

21 December 1963. The Queen with the Duke of Edinburgh, Princess Anne, Prince Andrew and one of the royal corgies at Liverpool Street station on their way to Sandringham for the Christmas holidays

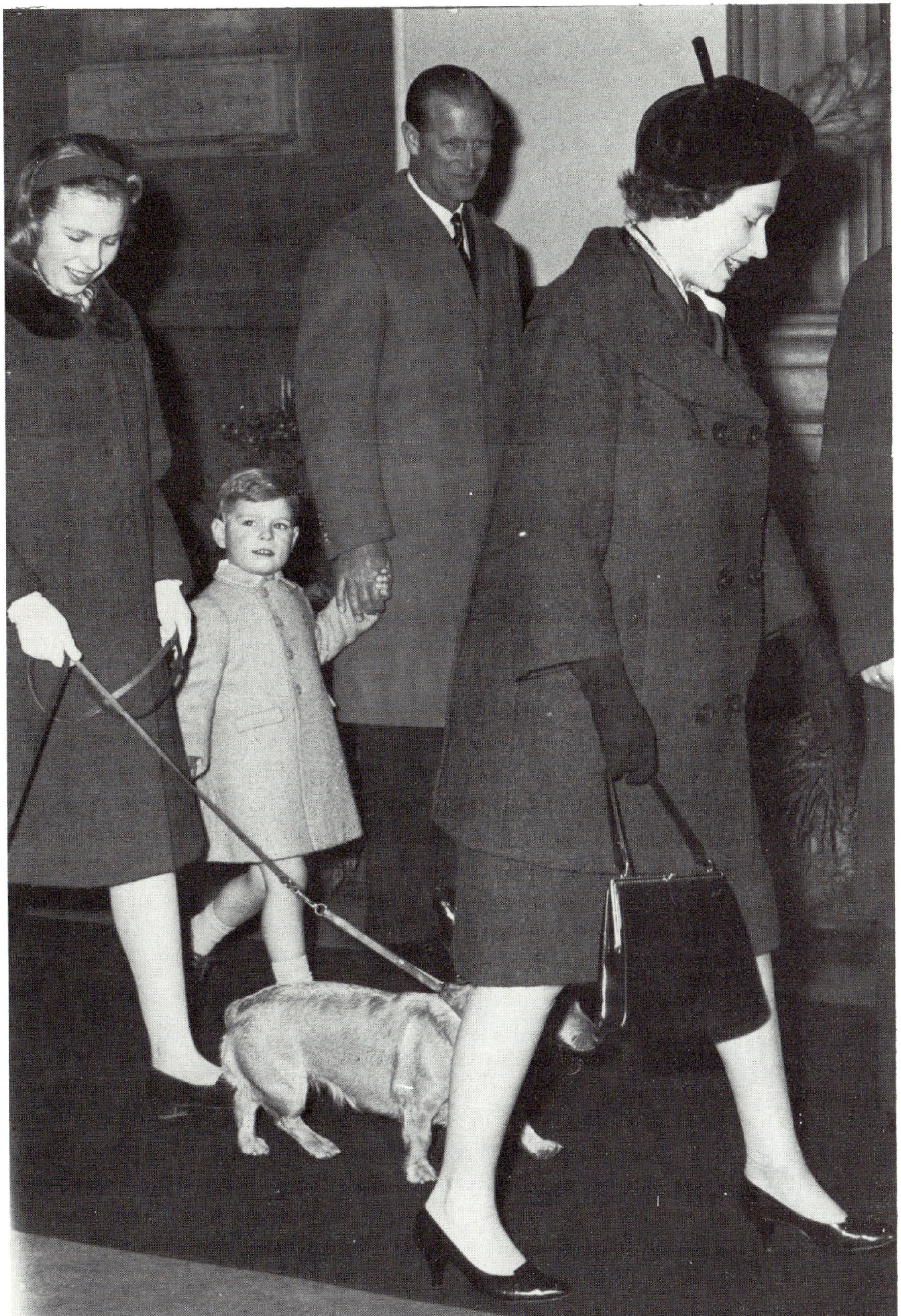

13 June 1964. Prince Edward, who was born on 10 March, surprised the crowds when he made his first public appearance on the balcony of Buckingham Palace after the Trooping of the Colour

Prince Andrew and nine-month-old Prince Edward on the train to Sandringham after spending Christmas at Windsor

58

8 November 1964. The Queen lays her wreath at the Cenotaph in London, in remembrance of the dead of both world wars. In the background, also carrying wreaths, are, from left to right, Mr Jo Grimond, Sir Alec Douglas-Home, Lord Attlee and the new Prime Minister, Mr Harold Wilson

22 May 1965. The Queen's State visit to Germany gave her a chance to meet some of Prince Philip's relations in their own homes. She is photographed here at Salem Castle, the home of Prince Philip's sister, Theodora, the Margravine of Baden (far right). On the Queen's left is Maximilian, Theodora's son, the present Margrave of Baden

Right. The Queen and Prince Philip in the grounds of Balmoral Castle. The picture was taken in 1972 at the time of their Silver Wedding anniversary

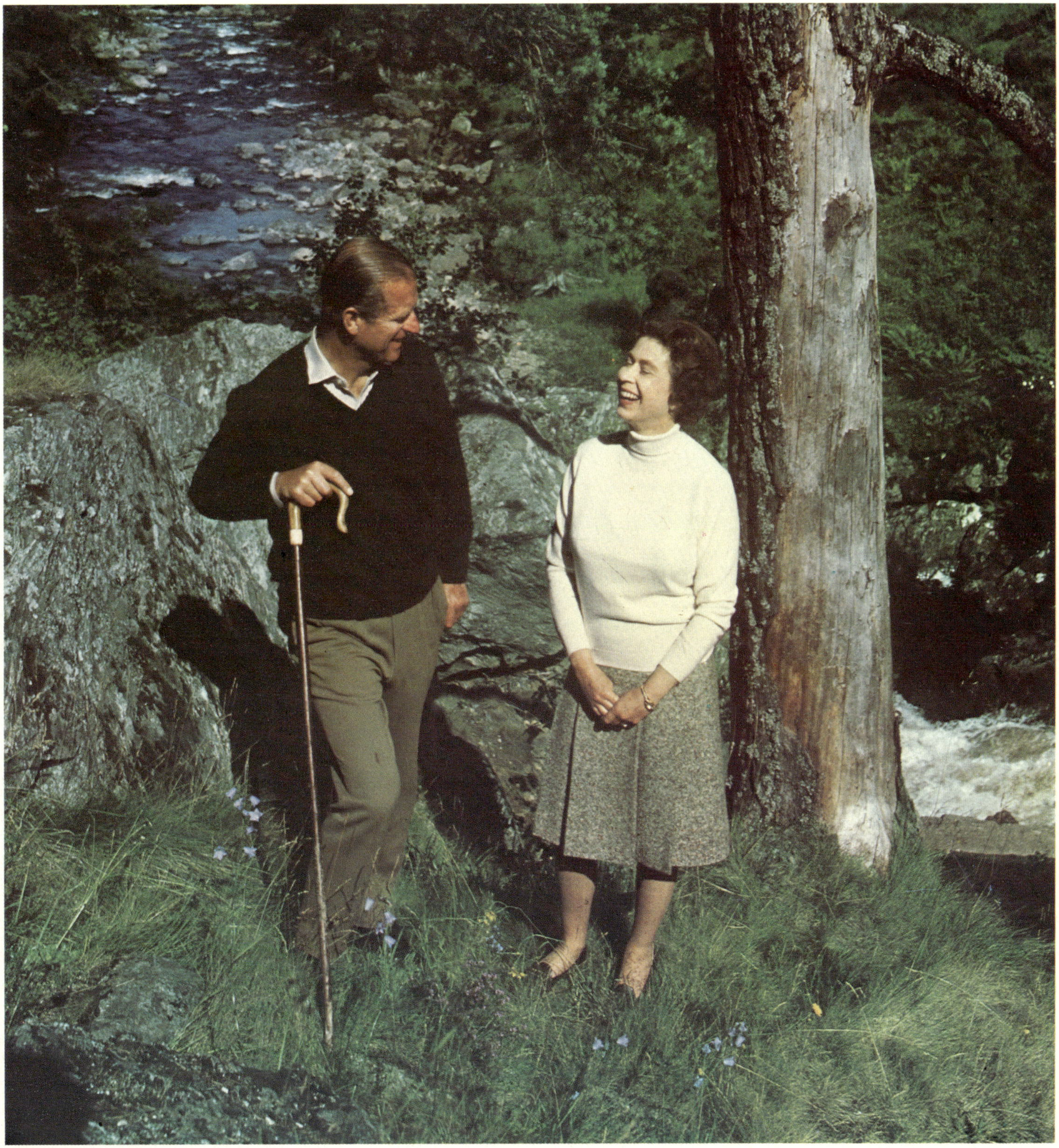

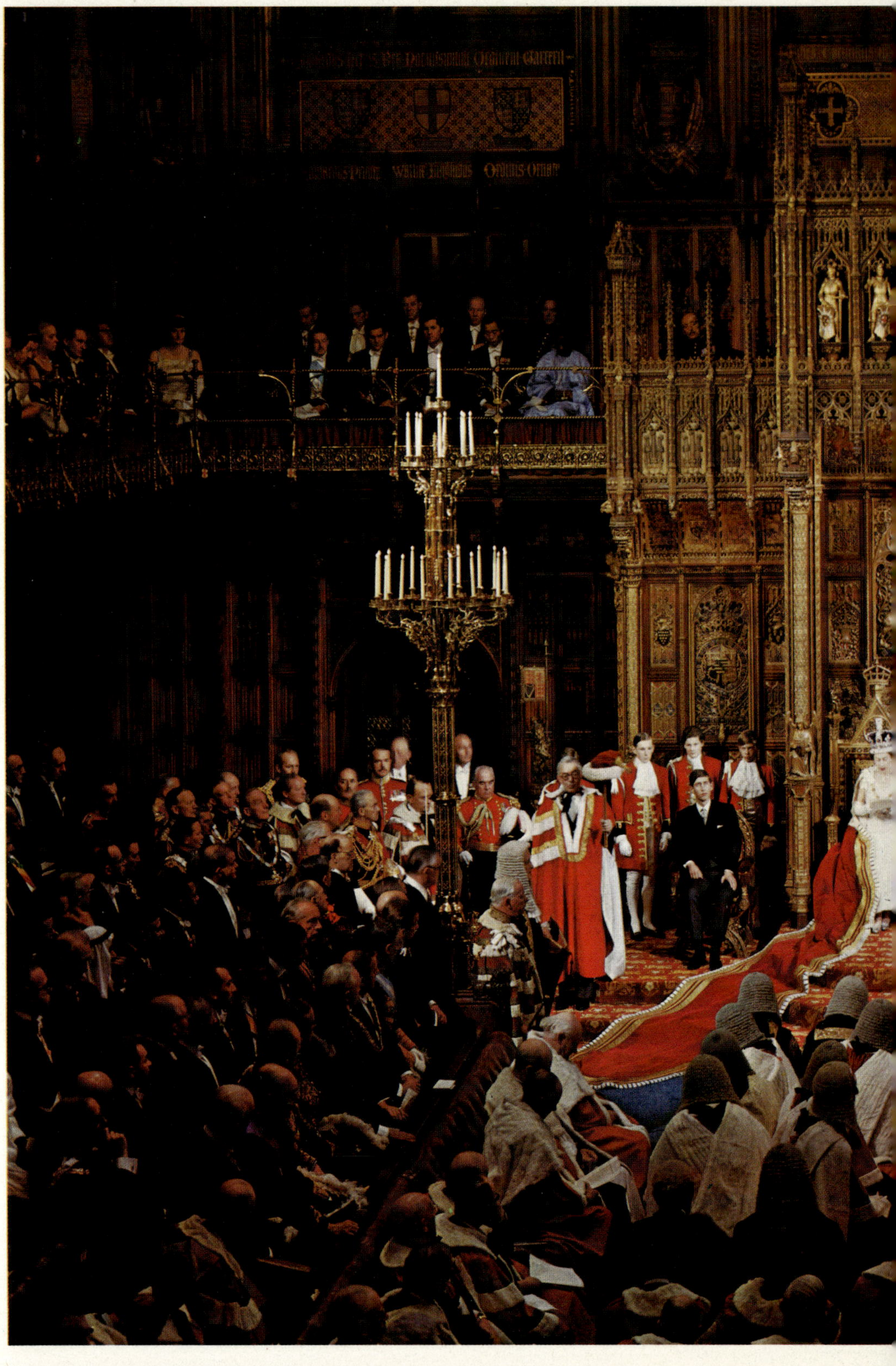

31 October 1967. The House of Lords during the State opening of Parliament. This was the first occasion that Prince Charles and Princess Anne were present

'One in the Eye.' The Queen, as guest of honour, dots the eyes of a ceremonial dragon during the royal visit to Hong Kong in 1975. Once his eyes are painted the dragon 'comes alive' and leads the rest of the carnival in a strenuous dance of welcome

February 1974. The Queen and Princess Anne admire straw hats given to them by Maori women at an open-air fair in Auckland, New Zealand

21 April 1966. State Opening of Parliament. The Queen, in evening dress and wearing the Imperial State Crown with its 3,093 jewels, receives her speech from the Lord Chancellor

7 July 1967. Sir Francis Chichester receiving the accolade of knighthood from the Queen at a ceremony held at Greenwich, following his lone yacht trip around the world. This ceremony recalled a similar occasion in 1581, when the first Queen Elizabeth knighted Francis Drake after he too had completed a round-the-world voyage

8 September 1966. On a visit to the Concorde project at the British Aircraft Corporation factory in Bristol, the Queen is shown a scale model of the supersonic aeroplane

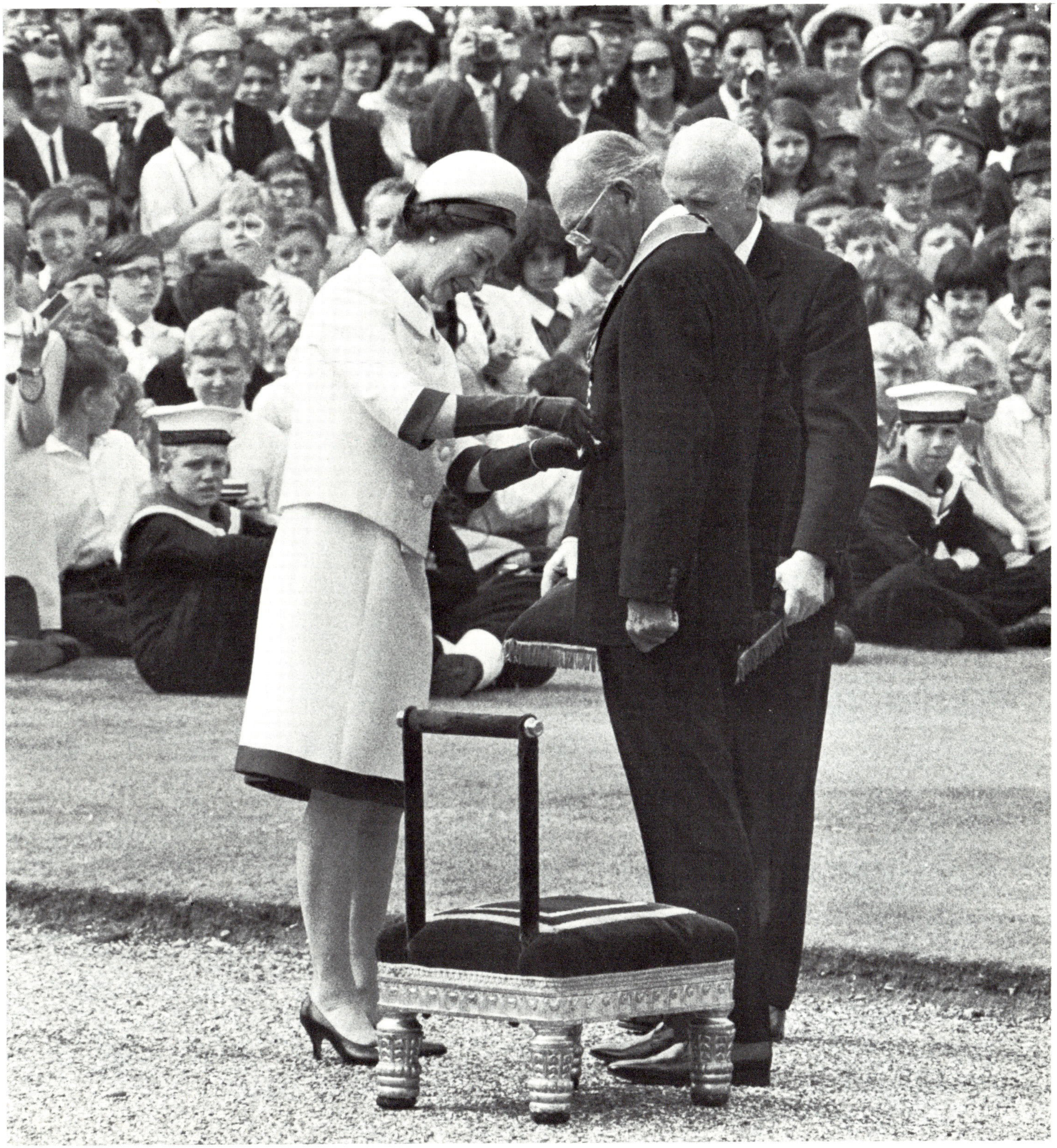

The Queen is constantly meeting a wide variety of famous people. As head of State she entertains statesmen and politicians like Mr Kosygin, the Russian Premier, seen here with his daughter at Buckingham Palace. As a patron and supporter of many charity ventures the Queen comes into contact with the many show business celebrities who give their services to raise money. Here (*left*) she talks to Welsh singer, Tom Jones. Also in the picture are Ken Dodd, Mireille Mathieu, Vicki Carr and Val Doonican

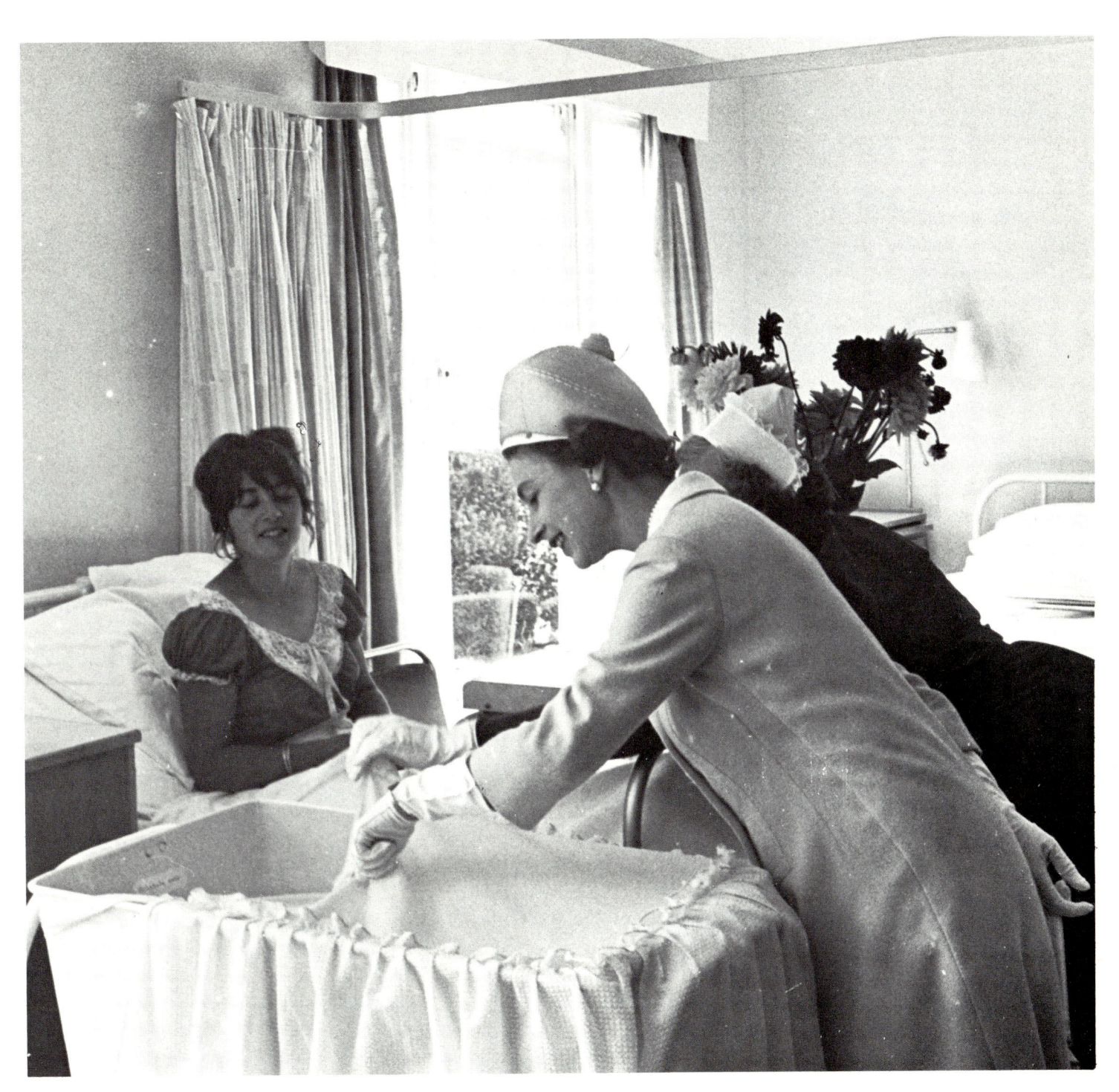

8 August 1967. During her visit to the hospital at St Mary's in the Isles of Scilly, the Queen peeps into the cot of her namesake, Elizabeth-Ann Ellis, born only thirty-six hours earlier. The baby's proud mother looks on

16 November 1967. The Queen and Prince Philip at a ball held in Valetta during the State visit to Malta

26 June 1968. A charming close-up of the Queen at the Royal Commonwealth Society's centenary garden party at Marlborough House

The Queen's sporting family

3 August 1968. Princess Anne receives a rosette from her mother at the Eridge Horse Trials. Princess Anne, like her husband Captain Mark Phillips, now specializes in three-day eventing. In 1971 she won the Individual European Three-Day Event at Burghley and was voted Sportswoman of the Year

20 July 1969. The most coveted trophy of the polo world, the Cowdray Gold Cup, is presented by the Queen to her husband whose team, Windsor Park, have just defeated their opponents 7–6 in the final. The Duke has now given up polo in favour of four-in-hand driving and is already a competitor of international standard. The polo-playing tradition is now continued by Prince Charles

May 1971. The Queen and Prince Philip, with Prince Edward (right), chat to spectators of the coaching marathon in Windsor Great Park. The Queen has more pressures on her privacy than any of her predecessors and riding is an ideal way of relaxing away from the crowds

1 July 1969. Caernarvon Castle. Prince Charles is invested as the twenty-first Prince of Wales and makes the same oath of allegiance his father did at the coronation. The tradition of making the Heir Apparent Prince of Wales goes back to 1301, when Edward I gave the title to his son. Before the investiture Prince Charles took a term away from Cambridge to go to the University College of Wales where he studied Welsh. Here the Queen presents her son to the people at the Water Gate of the castle

July 1969. In a busy year which included the investiture and a special television film about the royal family the Queen and her family unwind in the rural atmosphere of Sandringham

The Queen in contrasting headgear.
(*top*) Wearing a protective helmet on a visit to the Basic Oxygen Steelmaking Plant at Port Talbot, South Wales, in 1970;
(*below*) a very feminine creation, in keeping with the surroundings at the Chelsea flower show in 1967

7 May 1970. During the royal tour of
Australia the Queen is introduced to some
koala bears during a visit to Brisbane

May 1971. With Prince Edward and her niece, Lady Sarah Armstrong-Jones, the Queen watches the teams at the water-splash section of the International Driving Grand Prix in Windsor Great Park

August 1971. The royal family visits an Army display and exhibition at Aldershot.
Left to right: Prince Charles, Princess Anne, the Duke of Edinburgh, Prince Andrew, Prince Edward, the Queen. Her Majesty is the head of all the country's armed forces

5 October 1971. His Imperial Majesty, the Emperor Hirohito of Japan, and his wife Empress Nagako stand with the Queen in the Music Room of Buckingham Palace, before going in to a State banquet in their honour. The Emperor is wearing the insignia of the Order of the Garter, restored to him a few months earlier

12 August 1971. The Queen and her family pay a visit to one of the remotest parts of the United Kingdom, the island of St Kilda in the Outer Hebrides

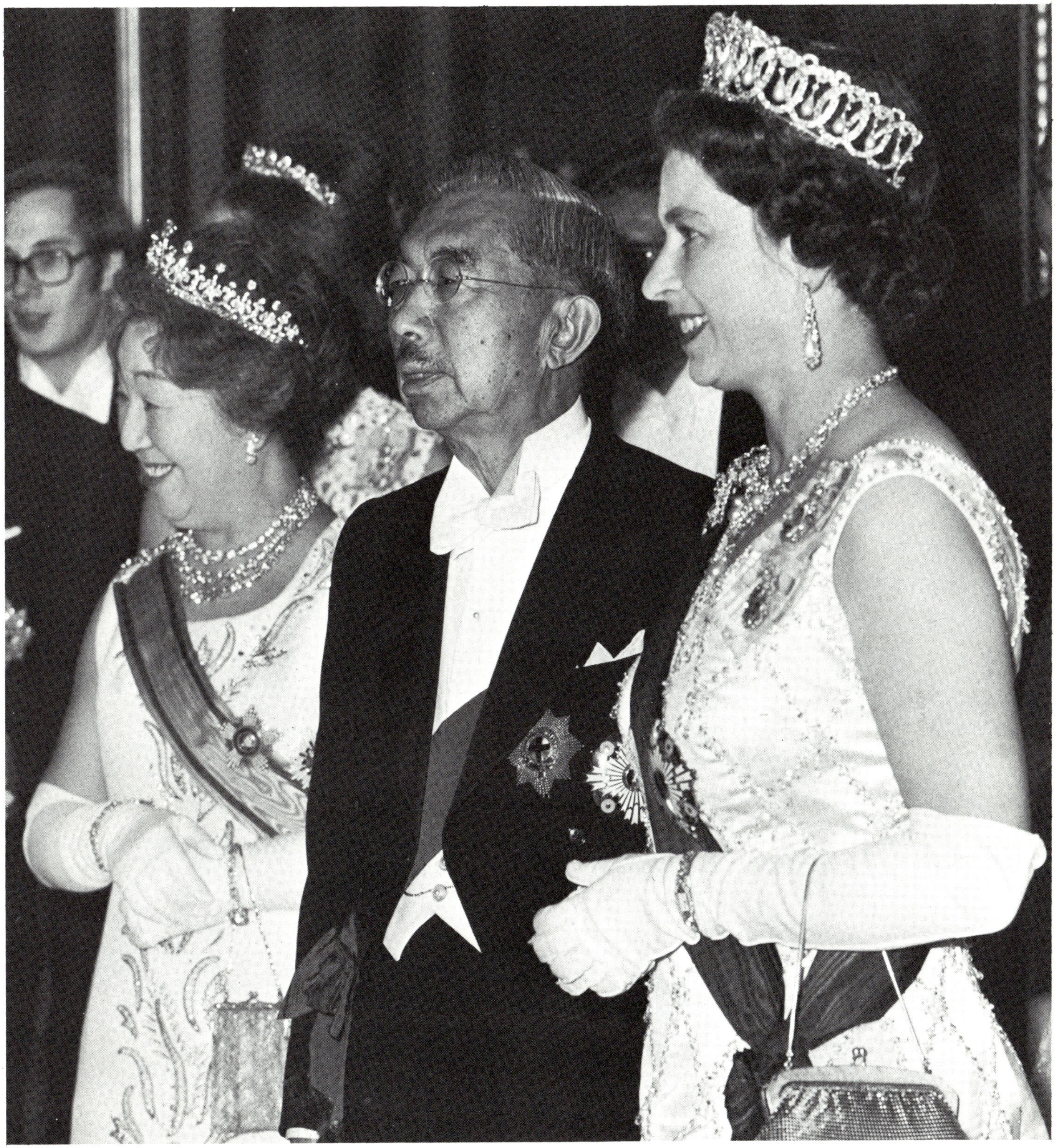

5 June 1972. The Queen and the Duke of Edinburgh pause for a word with the Duchess of Windsor outside St George's Chapel, Windsor, after the funeral service of the Duke of Windsor who died on 28 May

5 July 1972. The Royal Show, Kenilworth. One of the prize winners at the show was the Queen's *Windsor Louise's Polyanthus*, here being admired by her owner. Wherever possible the Queen's estates are run as economic agricultural units. Sandringham has 20,000 acres of valuable farming land. Windsor provides most of the vegetables, fruit and flowers required by the royal household as well as butter for the royal breakfast table

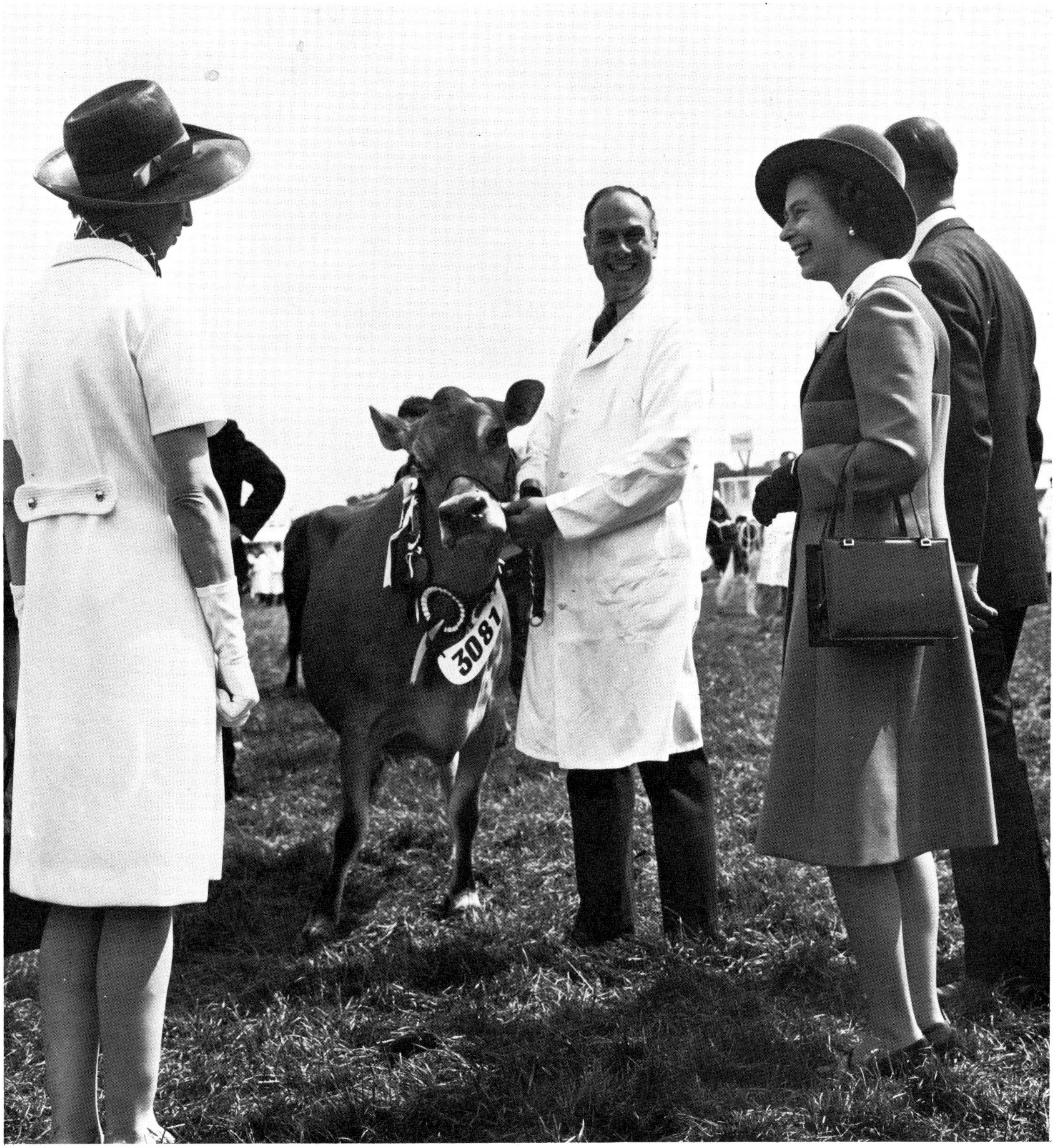
3081

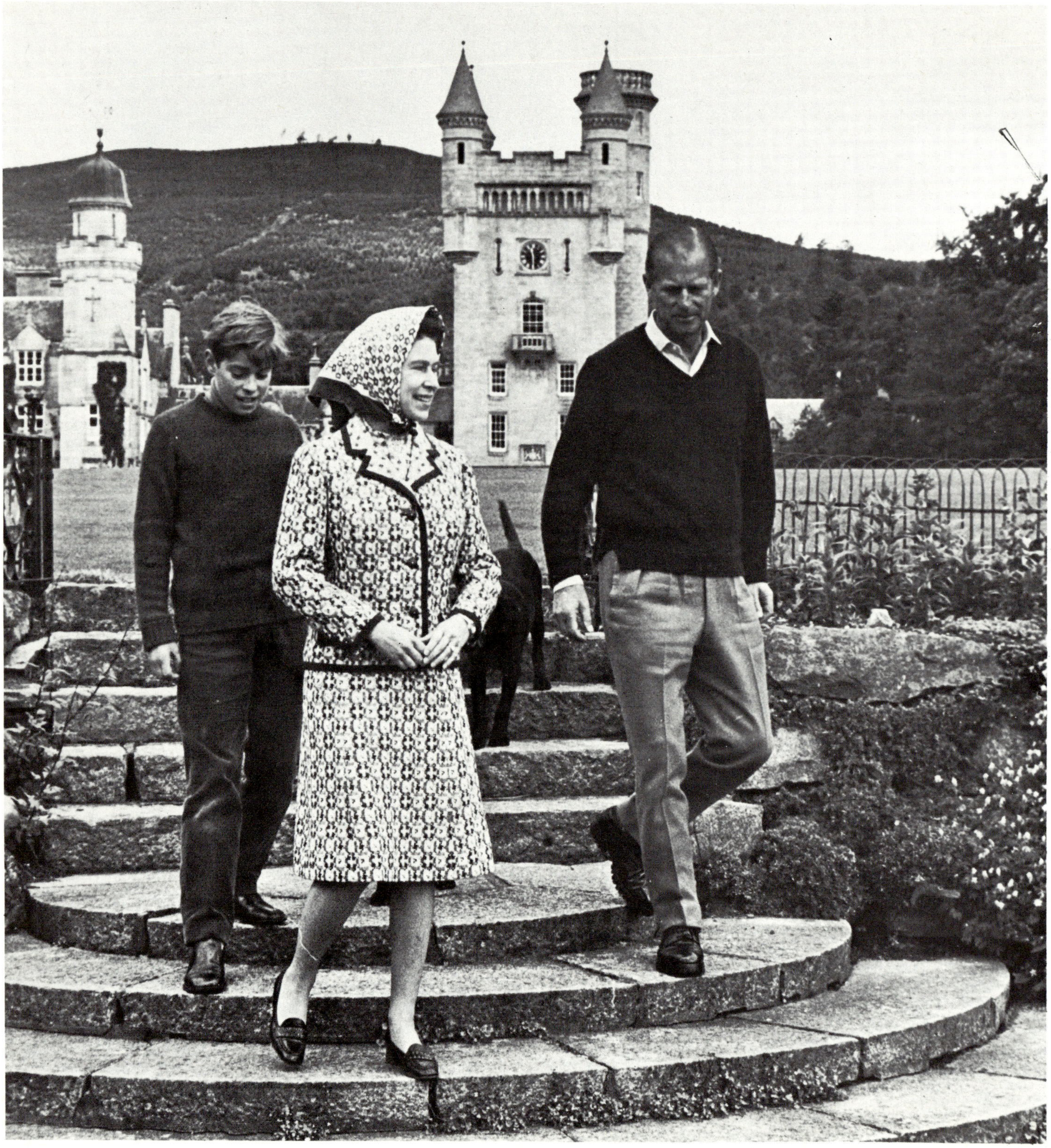

The Queen and the Duke of Edinburgh celebrated their Silver Wedding anniversary on 20 November 1972. The occasion was marked by a special service in Westminster Abbey on the day itself, and by a series of informal photographs taken at Balmoral Castle

Left. The Queen and the Duke walking in the grounds of Balmoral with Prince Andrew

The Queen, the Duke of Edinburgh, Prince Charles and Princess Anne leaving Buckingham Palace in an open carriage for the anniversary service in Westminster Abbey

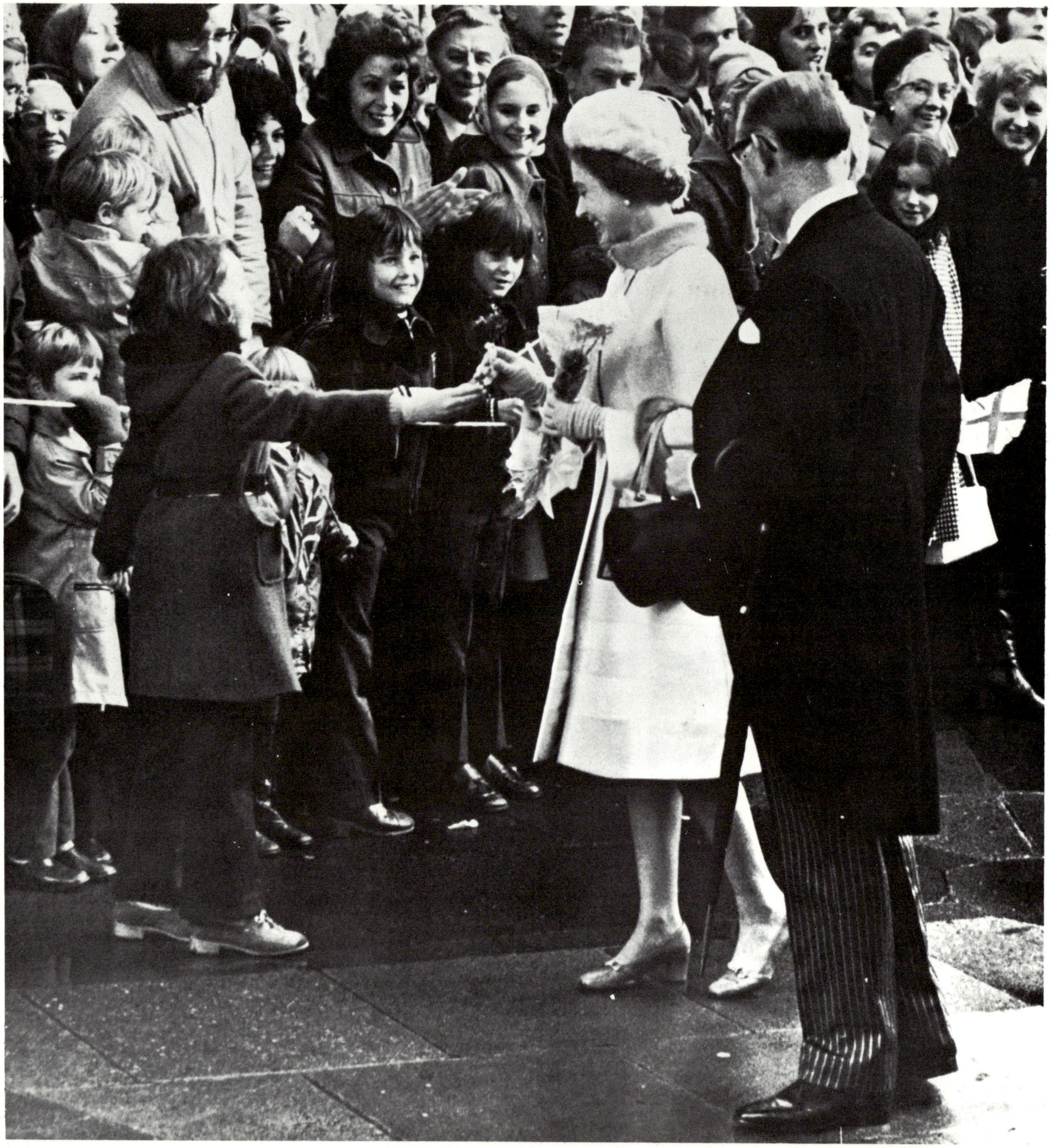

Left. Later in the day, after the pageantry and ceremony of the morning, the Queen went on an informal 'walkabout' in the City to meet the people of London. During her half-mile walk the Queen was greeted by hundreds of well-wishers

The Queen and the Duke toast each other at a luncheon given by the City of London in the Guildhall as part of the Silver Wedding celebrations

Even when on holiday in Scotland the Queen has to deal with State papers which are sent to her every day. Here she is at her desk on which stands a photograph of her father with Prince Charles

6 March 1973. The Queen repeats the informal 'walkabout' which was a popular feature of her Silver Wedding celebrations, after opening the new London Bridge

12 May 1973. After watching the Duke of
Edinburgh competing in the European
Driving Championships, the Queen, clutching
a handful of leads, entices her dogs to heel

27 July 1972. The Queen and the Queen Mother arriving at Westminster Abbey for the wedding of Lady Elizabeth Anson, daughter of Princess Georg of Denmark, with Sir Geoffrey Shakerley. At this wedding Princess Anne played the part of bridesmaid for the sixth time

Right. 11 September 1973. Prince Andrew arrives with his parents at Gordonstoun School where Prince Charles had been a pupil from 1962 to 1967. The school, which places great emphasis on physical fitness, was founded shortly before World War II by the German educationalist Kurt Hahn. Prince Philip, who had been to Hahn's first school at Salem in Germany, was one of its first pupils

28 December 1972. The Queen and the Duke with their youngest son, Prince Edward, at Liverpool Street station

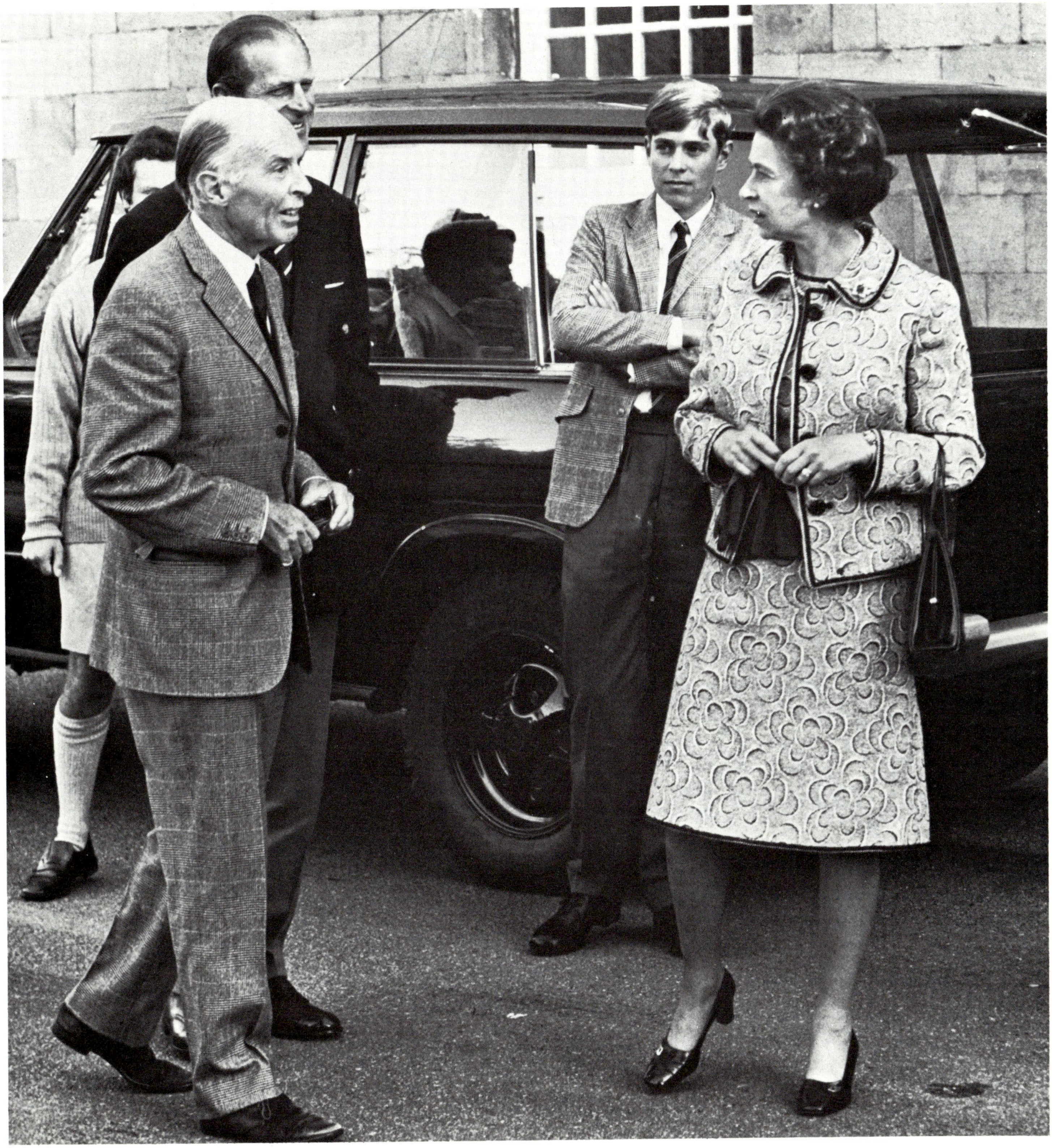

14 November 1973. The wedding of Princess Anne and Captain Mark Phillips at Westminster Abbey. The photograph is a family group taken by Norman Parkinson in the throne room at Buckingham Palace

1 Princess Beatrix of the Netherlands; 2 Ex-King Constantine of Greece; 3 Prince Claus of the Netherlands (husband of Princess Beatrix); 4 Ex-Queen Anne-Marie of Greece; 5 Miss Sarah Phillips; 6 Mr Peter Phillips; 7 Mrs Peter Phillips; 8 The Duchess of Kent; 9 Princess Alexandra; 10 The Hon. Angus Ogilvy (husband of Princess Alexandra); 11 Captain Eric Grounds (Best Man); 12 The Duke of Edinburgh; 13 Princess Richard of Gloucester; 14 Prince Richard of Gloucester; 15 The Duke of Kent; 16 Prince Charles; 17 The Earl Mountbatten of Burma; 18 Princess Sophie of Greece (wife of Prince Juan Carlos); 19 Prince Andrew; 20 Prince Juan Carlos of Spain; 21 Prince Michael of Kent; 22 Princess Alice, Countess of Athlone; 23 Crown Prince Harald of Norway; 24 Crown Princess Sonja of Norway; 25 Captain Mark Phillips; 26 Princess Anne; 27 The Queen; 28 The Duchess of Gloucester; 29 Queen Elizabeth, The Queen Mother; 30 Princess Margaret, Countess of Snowdon; 31 The Earl of Snowdon; 32 James Ogilvy; 33 Prince Edward; 34 Lady Sarah Armstrong-Jones; 35 Marina Ogilvy; 36 Viscount Linley; 37 Lady Helen Windsor; 38 The Earl of St Andrews

4 February 1974. The Queen in her role as Queen of New Zealand opens the New Zealand parliament at Wellington. With her are the Duke of Edinburgh, Prince Charles, Princess Anne and Princess Anne's husband, Captain Mark Phillips, on his first major royal tour since his marriage

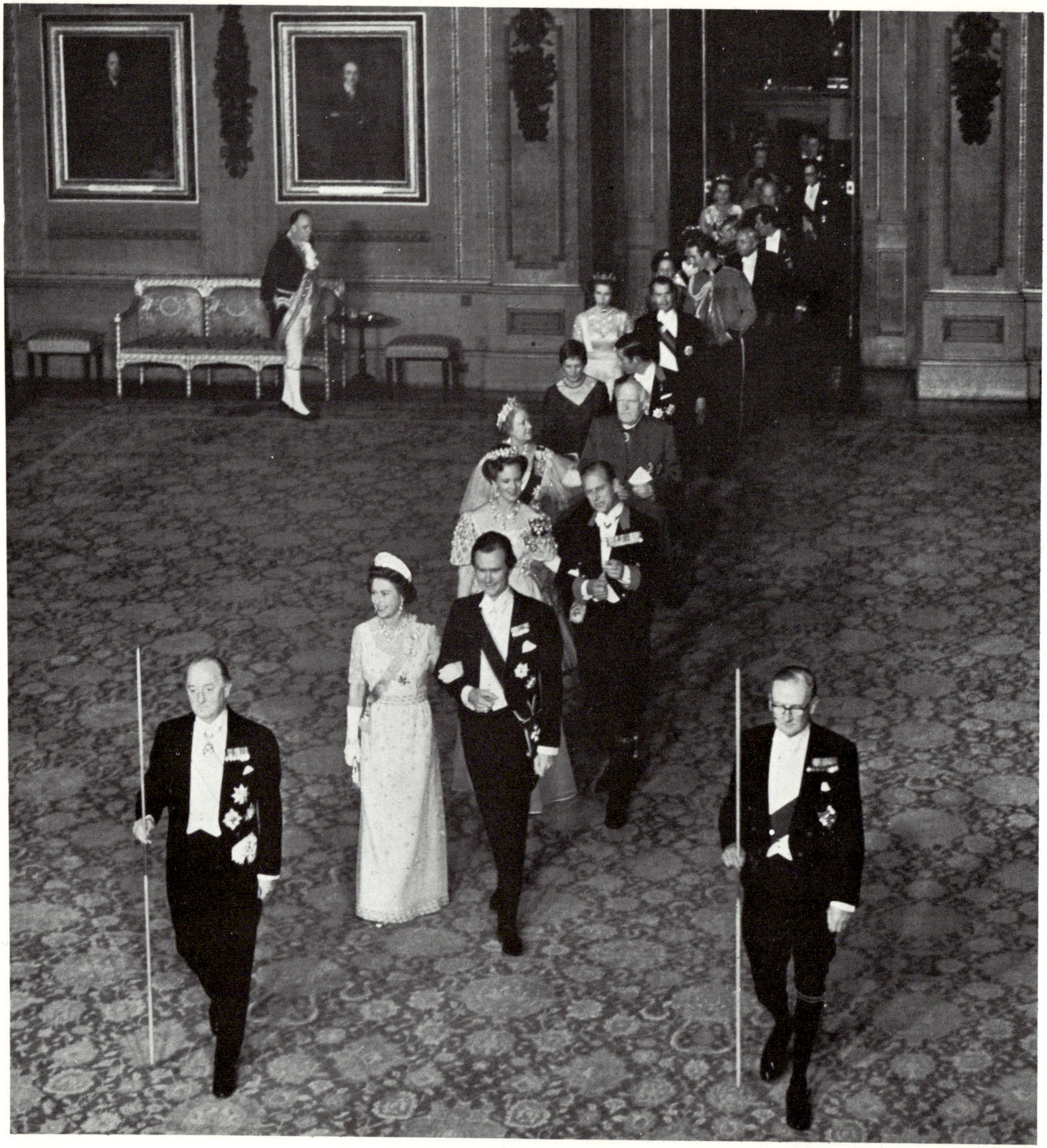

30 April 1974. The Queen and the Duke of Edinburgh gave a State banquet at Windsor for Queen Margrethe II and the Prince of Denmark, Prince Henrik. Queen Elizabeth and Prince Henrik lead the procession from the reception room to St George's Hall where the banquet was held.

State banquets have all the elegance and formality of a bygone era and the fairytale atmosphere is enhanced by the fact that the meal is eaten off solid gold plate

The Queen and Prince Philip chatting with Queen Margrethe and Prince Henrik in the Grand Reception Room at Windsor Castle. Prince Philip wears court dress with the Garter on his left leg

The Queen's dark blue velvet cloak is caught by the breeze as she emerges from St George's Chapel, Windsor, after the traditional Garter Ceremony. On the cloak is the Garter Star, a gift from her father, George VI. The Most Noble Order of the Garter, which is limited to twenty-four knights and a small number of royal princes and foreign monarchs, is one of the few orders in the Queen's personal gift

28 May 1975. Prince Charles and the Queen enter Westminster Abbey, where the Prince is to be installed as a Member of the Most Honourable Order of the Bath. Prince Charles, who flew back from a naval exercise in Canada for the ceremony, still sports a moustache

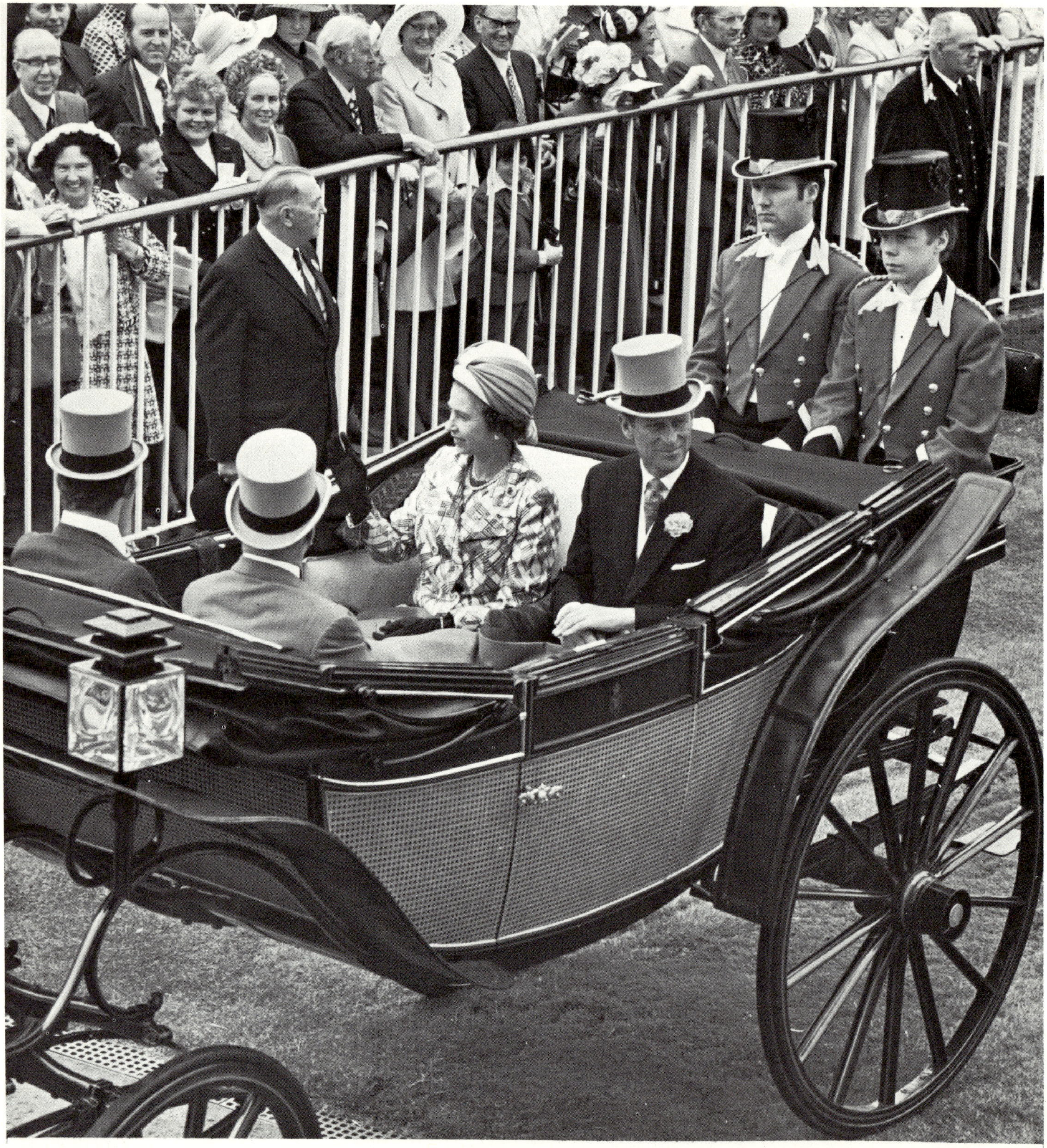

19 June 1974. On the second day of Royal Ascot the Queen and the Duke of Edinburgh, with the Master of the Queen's Horse, drive along the course. Royal Ascot was begun by Queen Anne, a keen horsewoman, at the beginning of the eighteenth century. Queen Elizabeth still owns the course but takes no revenue from it

11 July 1974. Her Majesty with her bodyguard of the Yeomen of the Guard in the garden of Buckingham Palace

May 1975. The Queen's State visit to Japan. Her Majesty visits an exhibition of flower arranging in Tokyo. The exhibition was constructed to resemble a typical Japanese house and the fragile bamboo floors required the removal of shoes

In Kyoto the Queen sat on the floor and used chopsticks to eat a Japanese meal given for her by the Japanese Society. With the traditional food the Queen drank saké, Japanese rice wine

May 1975. On her four-day tour of Hong Kong the Queen visited one of the colony's thriving street markets. The expedition was not on the official schedule and the Queen surprised everyone with her early morning arrival to see this typical Hong Kong scene for herself

The Queen travelling on one of Japan's famous 125mph trains

Acknowledgements

I should like to record my appreciation of the assistance I have had from the Buckingham Palace Press Office who were always helpful and quick to answer my queries; and Mr Bill Hulme of Fox Photos who was so helpful in finding all the pictures I required from the millions of photographs in their library.

M.B.